Why Life is So Queer

Is life a result of random acts?

By Vasant Prasad

Neither the author nor the publisher assumes any responsibility or liability whatsoever on the behalf of the purchaser or reader of these materials.

Any perceived slight of any individual or organization is purely unintentional.

FIRST EDITION

Table of Contents

Introduction

What do you think, my friend?

Is life all prewritten story? Or, on the other hand, is it a chain of totally random events?

This random thought or question may have come to you in a flash at least once in your life. Or it must have crossed your mind, at least, at a time when things were going all wrong.

You take anything in life, there are two sides. Some of us look to the left and others look to the right.

Leftists say it's all pre-defined and planned in life. Nothing is by accident.

Rightists say no, no, it's not predefined at all, not at all. Life is just too random. Nothing is pre-determined.

As humans, we continue to be divided. Each side has a lot of good and loyal companies.

What you're reading here is my view of the random nature of life. Life teaches us a lot all through our living. What I write here is based on my observations and experiences of life over the years.

Here, at the beginning of this book itself, you met RANDOMNESS, wasn't it? How is that?

Now that you are reading my book, this is in itself a better example of what I'm going to talk about in this book.
Did you pick this book up by random chance or was it predefined? There is whole lot of books out there in the world. But how did you choose this book?

 Is my book not a RANDOM pick?

I will refer back to this example later in the book.

It's my attempt to see events in life through the lens of randomness!!!

For those who look to the right- Life is all random occurrences.

You are interested in the topic and willing to go deep and know all there is to know about it, a **dilettante**. The points I make all through this book may appeal to you and may change the way you look and think about life. Accepting and learning to deal with randomness of life can even change the way you live your life. Maybe, you will enjoy the happier and more successful life. You may be less depressed and sad in life than ever before.

If you embrace this idea and begin to understand it, you have my advice in the sub-topic "What Randomness means to you?" at the end of this book.

For those who look to the left- Life is prewritten story

You don't believe in Randomness. Right, you are going the other way and you're looking at things from left. You are taking snaps of life, shot from the other side (left). Your slant is nothing is ever random.

That's why your views are just as important. I used to look from your side before but I caved in.

Nothing is right or wrong here. However, here is my caveat for you, to read this book with your mind wide open and think about the points I am laying out all through this book.

Why blind your eyes for a few specific colors, see life in full and true color!!!

Maybe you're right in more than one way.

However, to discover the real picture, at least something close to the real if not completely true, you need to see the picture of both sides, right?

Know that even the randomness that is generated in science and mathematics is pseudo, not really random.

Taste all my words and all that I say from now on. Let me know what taste this book leaves when I finish it.

This book looks at these questions

- How to accept life?
- Why life is not predictable?
- Can success be repeated?
- Who influences and shapes our destiny?
- What Randomness means to you
- What you can do about it

Let's get down to the matter.

Yes, I know I've started writing about something, Randomness of life, which can start a debate or an argument. Yet the matter is quite curious and interesting enough to read to the end.

The curtain will go UP now.

Just be alert and follow me along.

The flow begins from here on....

What is this Random anyway?

Many of us are haunted by this idea - is random real or does it not exist?

By RANDOM, I mean something that has no particular order or rules to follow and that is completely accidental and by chance. There is no pattern at all and is not repeatable or regular. We can be **certain** that life is out-and-out **UNCERTAIN**. **It looks just as chaotic**. Randomness and chaos are good friends!

You may have played the random spinning wheel game. You may've thrown or rolled a dice in the games. You may have tossed a coin. You will get to know an idea of the true randomness in all of these.

I am not using the word random here in the same sense as that used in mathematics, science or computer science. Even the randomness generated in these fields is not random in the true sense of the word, it is pseudo-random or it appears random enough!

It is in this sense, I say that life is a chain of RANDOM EVENTS. Events just happen, and nobody controls them.

Many things are random and chaotic in nature in the universe. We go through random events everyday. It is random because of the complexity and chaos of the universe.

In life, what we don't know is a lot more than what we know.

The unknown is way more than the known. What is invisible is far more than visible.

The equations in life have a lot of unknowns.

That's why these random sequences of events have amazing or worst possibilities in this world and specifically, in my life and in yours.

You may scoff at these and say why then a new world or a new planet is not created by random events now as in the past. Why is no new thing created?

It's so confusing and misleading, isn't it? Hold ON!

Remember that there are still many things in the world that follow the rules and laws of the universe. Events have causes and effects as well. Events may also have scientific reasons but they do have a time element. However, it is the time of events or their occurrence is random. That's the point I'm making. This timing has a profound impact on our life. More often, you experience this timing of events. Take for example; you are just about to start from home for shopping. However, somewhere in the sea the air pressure drops and it begins to rain in your area. Yes, there's a scientific reason for this rain. But the point is why this should happen when you were on your way out? The timing of the event is what makes it random.

Let's look at some examples that don't seem random but are follow certain rules. The movements of stars and planets, the cycle of seasons all follow certain laws of the universe and may be predictable to some degree. However, even these can be affected and upset at any time by an event!

You know this well. There are many things in this world that follow the laws of universe. And a lot more things that are purely random. The two coexist in the universe. For this reason, it appears predefined sometimes and randomly most other times.
That should be enough to mislead you to think anyway, right?

Random logic is more like the logic of induction. If an answer can provide a possible explanation for many of our observations, then that could be right.
The idea or answer I'm speaking about here is the sequence of Radom events. This concept explains much of what we observe in life.

Life is already too complex to even think about comprehension because of the large number of unknown and obscure factors. Randomness adds even more to take it a way beyond our discovery. Everything in life seems to be well kept secret and will not let anybody in on its secrets.

Why do you think that is? We call all that we cannot understand and explain is a well kept secret. By its very nature, randomness is mysterious and elusive ever. It's something that pops up all of a sudden out of the blue. That's more like a blackout. It does not allow you to have a bit or an iota of clue.

So, as I would see it, it is this randomness that gives life a look and feel of something not understandable, not explainable, and not discoverable ever or hard-to-crack secret, so to speak. That makes life a puzzle.

Perhaps you are now beginning to perceive why everything is thus covert in everyday life?

Henry Adams (a well-known American historian and journalist) aptly says –

"Chaos was the law of nature; Order was the dream of man."

How it possibly works?

I have been talking about random events. I would like to expand on these events further.

When I say events, I mean one of the two types. First, the events started or were created by you. Second, events caused by outside or external influences.

Remember, the two events are just as RANDOM as your thoughts!!!

Your Events -

You keep creating events all through the day for a lot of reasons. You are thinking all the time, aren't you? Thoughts keep popping up in your mind. Mind is always active and in action. Your random thoughts lead you to some action. Even your passion drives you into action. Your actions may or may not be planned. These actions are events you created and started. Say, you have to attend an interview and you started out.

External events -

External events are just all happenings in your proximity or anywhere in the world. These events can occur at random anywhere in the world. Worse yet, they are not under anyone's control.

Let me continue with the same example of your attending an interview.

You're on your way to interview- it's your event. Now there are a lot many possibilities of external events that can happen- a traffic jam, a downpour, an accident, your vehicle developing a problem, you are caught by traffic police etc. or many of these could be happening all at once!

These external events can have a huge impact on your first event, the one you started.

The following outcome can be anything, GOOD or BAD. This is just one example of mix of events.

Now imagine more events like this and the outcomes.

A whole lot of possibilities . . .

They can make you fall into ruin or pitch you up in life.

They may turn you into a hero or zero!!!

They can even destroy the good results of past events, making your life take a full U-turn!!!

Even someone's mistake can be a favorable event for you or your own incorrect choice can be an event that can begin your downfall.

And more and more possibilities . . .

By random chance, a fatal illness may develop in your body.
A person can suddenly have a heart attack, a cerebral hemorrhage, or a stroke. All these are random possibilities.

You and I have seen all of these, haven't we?

Covid-19 is a good example of an event happening in a far away location and its impact on other parts of the world, to cite here. You probably have unforgettable experiences and lessons from this event. The entire world, businesses, your life, my life and all aspects of life in general have been completely affected. Covid-19 began in a far-off region of the world. But this external event has touched and affected every corner of the globe. Some businesses have gone out of business. Some of us have lost our jobs!

Do you see the unstoppable BIG power of external event?

You now know what I mean by external events and the ones you started. Let me explain these two events a little more.

Now imagine two sequences of random events cropping up together and intercepting one another-- one event started by you and the other is an external event. These intersections of events may be in your favor or they may work against you. Outcomes at these moments can be GOOD or BAD.

It is this series of criss-crossing events, occurring one after another, that make up your life. And the choices you make at the convergence of events have life-changing effect.

Crossing events can lead you to an unexpected and sudden fame or it can mean an abrupt end of life!

They can bring a more serious problem or a long-awaited solution to a long-running problem. They can even end the long suffering.

 I will come back to the example of you picking up this book here. You may be in some part of the world. You started searching for a book. This is one event. While you were searching, this book appeared in the search result. This is the second event. As a result of these crossing events, you picked it up and started reading it, didn't you? This is just a pure random matter.

Let me pick another example.
Have you ever played the **Snakes and Ladders game?** The game is also called **Chutes and Ladders. This game can give you an experience, close to the real life, of the crossing events I was talking. Play this game to get an idea of randomness. You can play it online too.**

It is a board game two or more players can play. The board has a grid of 100 square boxes, numbered from 1 to 100. There are few pictures of "ladders" and "snakes" in random locations on the board. Each ladder or snake connects two or more squares.

The goal of the player is to start from the first square box and reach the square numbered 100, the last box. Each player is represented by a game-piece. The player rolls the dice and keeps moving his game-piece to the 100th box based on the dice number. In his journey to the last box, the player may reach ladder or snake by random chance.
The ladders take the player up and help him move forward fast. The snakes, on the other hand, slow down the player, moving him downwards and backwards.

It's the game in short.
What is the underlying idea in this game? - Sheer randomness. Rolling the dice is an event you start as a player. Reaching the ladder or snake by chance is an external event. This crossing of events can take you up or down on the board. Series of these crossing events can make your journey to the destination, the last box, faster or slower.

Three Aspects of Events

Events have three aspects: what, which type and what time. They're all three randoms.

- **What**

What events are possible? It could be a meeting with a future life partner or a job interview or beginning a new job or a new business or an accident in life. That's what I mean by "What" part of an event.

- **Type**

Events can be good or bad. It can be favorable or unfavorable to you. Event can let you down or give you an extra boost in life. Event can often be deadly and disaster or life saver.

It can fail you or win you a jackpot. You may hit a big time or it can begin a terrible time. It can put you to sudden fame or shame. You have seen it all.

- **Time**

Time is the "When" aspect of the event. Timing of an event or when it happens isn't foreseeable or controlled.

The pace or the time interval at which events happen influences our lives. It can make our life go slow for some time or fast at other time.

All three aspects of the events make your life zig and zag or form a zigzag path of your life.

You are now beginning to see the random nature of life in everything, aren't you?

It's just how it is! That is how your life can get quirky at any time and all the time!

Do you know about chaos theory and the butterfly effect?

Butterfly effect means that a butterfly flapping its wings somewhere in Amazon rainforest in America can cause heavy rain or a hurricane or an earthquake in Japan or India!!!

You and I are going to see through this RANDOM LENS from now on in the sections that follow, some of our long established understandings or notions like **predictions, miracles, luck, fate, and destiny, one by one**.

Why Predictions Fail?

Random means, something inherently unpredictable. It suggests or connotes a random occurrence, a happening by chance. Life is all random events. Very much like a random spinner wheel game or a dice rolling game or a game of chance. Randomness seems to be the underlying principle of life. Where life takes you, you do not know, nor can you predict.

Predictions of the future go beyond humans. Even science and astrology more often fail to make predictions of any kind, short term or long term. Why think of predicting the future, we can't even predict what's going to happen in a moment.

Because life is a complex equation of the many unknowns, life will remain random, no matter how much scientific research we put into it. It is simply impractical for us to know large number of variables. The missing factors are still going to be there. Maybe science and chance may not go together well, do they?

Check the weather predictions. Sophisticated, though, scientific weather forecasts frequently fail.

Yet another example is trading in capital markets.
Most predictions go wrong here too.
Game and life look very similar in RANDOMNESS.
Predicting who will win or loose the game can surprise and shock you. It is the same with the life as well.

Do you think anyone could have predicted ghastly tragic incident of "**9/11**" in the United States or the recent COVID-19 outbreak?

Why Success is not Repeatable?

There are many successful and accomplished people in the world. Every one of them has a completely different success story. They're not the same at all!!!

Ironically, though, even if you follow in their footsteps, your success is not guaranteed. It does not repeat!!!

Even then, you see a lot of "How to be successful" books or the likes on the shelves out there.

Well, you may be capable. Maybe you may have all the necessary skills. You may be hard working. But to be successful, it takes something more-- being in the right place at the right time; that random combination?

The chain of random events that lead you to success in your life or in someone's life will always be random and will not be repeated.

.

Our Idea of Destiny and Doom

Let me pick over this notion of destiny here. Destiny is one of life's secrets. Of course, it is. But you want to know your destiny ahead, don't you?

You may be destined to become the richest and wealthiest person in the world or a successful business person, or a great scientist or anything for that matter.

A Multitude of questions, surround the idea of destiny.

Is destiny something chosen by anyone or GOD? Why would god write or write-off your destiny?

Why would GOD take charge of your life? He leaves you free and gives you freedom. He never spoils or favors anything.

Do you smack of randomness here? Well, It is! Of What?

The randomness of life drives you to destiny. Random happenings shape your future. Accidental events, occurring one after the other, make up your path to your destiny. It is a mix of events that brings a turning point and something that makes a BIG difference in your life.

It is, by series of random events in your life, you reach the destiny.

 You are there or you are so near or you simply have to wait a bit longer to be at that destiny!

You need not despair. Hold on! To know what you can do, read on…

You will find my advice in the section "What Randomness means to you" later in this book.

Why anything is Possible in this World?

The other day I read in a news paper that a MAN became a pregnant and gave birth to a baby! It was in a place the south of England.

The Indian Express news paper, April 29, 2020 edition, reported that a woman in India's UP state, gave birth to five babies!!!

A beggar at railway station becomes a super hit star singer overnight!

All these incidents seem unlikely and impossible, but they are made possible by the randomness of the world. Life is full of such shocking realities and continues to throw such surprises. You hear them or see them everyday all around you.

Random combination of myriad of things out there in this world can make such hard-to-believe and completely impossible things a reality. It's just that incredible and amazing world.

Anything can happen at any moment by chance in this world. Probably, it supports the saying "Nothing is impossible"!!!

Imagine you're in a crazy, chaotic traffic without a traffic cop. Don't you experience "anything is possible" in that traffic?

Life is simply that .It's like that chaotic, **free-for-all** traffic you were in, but the scale of life is a lot bigger. We have got to explore and know more about randomness.

Our Idea of Luck, Miracle and Fate

It was 7 o'clock in the evening. I was on my way back from the office in a car. And heavy rains and wind started. I was almost half way from home and driving alongside a park. A van was coming up to me on the other side and was just passing by me on the right side. All of a sudden, I heard a loud sound. A tall tree came down and fell onto the van. Since the van was taller and bigger than my car, the falling tree just leaned onto the van and stopped there. Oops! I was rescued from the fall of a tree which would otherwise have been a catastrophe!!!

What a coincidence and what a random occurrence! You call this LUCK?

It's just a RANDOM incident, an accident. If the result of the random event is good, we call it luck.
If something good happens unexpectedly and by chance, we call it LUCK, don't we?

One day, I was reading a newspaper. My eyes fell on a piece of writing about a deadly car accident. It stated the entire family: father, mother, son and the daughter, was in the car. Everyone in the car died except the 4 year old daughter. The car door opened on one side and the girl was thrown out and survived!

What an accidental or providential escape! We call it miracle?
In both of the cases above, it is random chance but we always have name for it- we call it LUCK or MIRACLE.
When you've done all you can but you feel you're very close to something you don't want to happen. And when you have left all your hopes, something happens by chance all of a sudden exactly at that very moment. The result of that event is completely unexpected and unlikely but it is what you desperately needed at that moment. That is miracle, right? Do you see randomness in action and smell it in all these?

We call the power that controls the events as FATE, the controller. However, nobody controls this randomness. These events just happen. Sometimes, we also call an event as FATE, in a negative sense, if the result of an event is bad.

Everyday we see or hear about these types of random incidents, but we don't see them as accidental events.

What Randomness Means to You?

You have read the book thus far. And you know now more about random things in life.

However, one aspect of random events, that no body has control on them, must be bothering you. I know that's what you're really worried about.

You may ask if there is no control on anything that happens, should you leave everything to chance and just wait then. No, not at all.

If you don't take action, nothing will change. To increase your chances of achieving your goal, you should keep to trying and working your way.

 Remember, all your attempts are events started by you. When your event crosses with external event, the end result may be the U-turn of your life!!!

Well then, adopt the idea that randomness is there every step of your way.

So I have three tips to offer you to deal with the bumps of random events in life.

Here is my three apt tips- A.P.T

1. **Accept (A)**

    Randomness is the way of life. So accepting the randomness of life as the truth will set right your outlook and your expectations of life. It will make you strong when an event pulls you down and fails you. This can help you move ahead on the path you have chosen, undaunted and unwavering. You will be more level-headed while facing the oddities and weirdness of life.

2. **Positive Mindset (P) and Patience**

    The result of an event may not be in your favor and it may not be what you expected. A positive mindset, in that case, can keep your spirit and keep you going. You never can tell. You just don't know. You may be closer to your destiny or whatever you want. That one next event may change everything and make all the difference in your life.

Expect that the result will not be guaranteed to be a success all the time because of this randomness in life. Look at life this way.

If you fail in spite of your best effort, you need not despair. You have nothing to give up. It is not your fault, and you know why. Maybe this random event said "NO" to what you wanted. But, keep your hope and stick with life. The next event may say "YES" and may not let you down.

Have **inexhaustible or unlimited patience and positivity**. Continue to move forward with faith and the expectation that one little event will flip your life around. That's what is required most in the world of uncertainty.

3. Try, Try and Try (T)

It is easy to draw a parallel between the game of rummy cards and life. That's a great example. You know this game, perhaps. What do you do in this game? You continue to pick up and discard cards from the pile of cards face-down until you make a right combination of cards in your hand.

You pick, pick and pick cards to make the right sequence and you win. In life, you try, try and try until you hit upon the right sequence of events that brings a turning point.

Persevere and continue to try. Don't quit and sit. Don't be lazy and wait for the event to occur while you move on. Your job is to play your part well and give your all. Maybe you're so near to your destiny. It may take few or more events to reach your destiny and get what you wanted. If you continue to make more attempts, you increase your chances of encountering an event in your life that gets you success. Just one random event may be enough to change the direction of your life.

Hold on to what you have set out to achieve and don't give up your chase. I am sure your chase will end with an event that holds the key to your success.

Bear in mind, life takes you on an emotional roller coaster as it moves from event to event with all its randomness. Every event may not give what you want but one little random event can get you everything.

Until you meet with that event, try everything and give your all to chase your goal. Be ready to run a marathon just in case!

Look at these quotes from two great inspiring individuals - Albert Einstein and Nick Vujicic, just right for mentioning at this moment. Listen to these people here in their own words-

Albert Einstein

"You never fail until you stop trying."

Nick Vujicic

"If I fail, I try again, and again, and again."

Conclusion

Thank you, my friend. You followed my writing to the end. I hope it was good reading experience and my message was pretty clear. Before I conclude, I echo my message one last time so you remember.

I say your future is decided by yourself. You aim for something and begin your chase. The choice you make is very important. To make the right choice for yourself, it is very essential to be well informed. Along the way in your life, some events may block your progress. But, never mind, keep going. Events that follow may pave the way for you and turn your life around!!!

The twists and turns or ups and downs of life are the outcomes of a series of random events at work. So do not be discouraged by the turn of events in your life at any moment.

You will meet with that event sooner!

Your feedbacks and comments are of value to me.

You will inspire me to write more books.

Please leave your comments or a review on AMAZON, if you feel that this book holds something of value and something for you to follow.

Wish you best of everything- health and wealth, in life.

Thank you and Bye

Vasant Prasad

About the Author

Vasant Prasad is from India and lives in a city called **Bangalore**.

He loves a lot of things: technology, training, writing, copywriting, music, songs……

He holds an engineering degree. He has vast experience for over 25 years and has worked in both engineering and IT companies.

You can reach me on vasantprasad2002@yahoo.com

www.ingramcontent.com/pod-product-compliance
Lightning Source LLC
Chambersburg PA
CBHW071241240726
48654CB00009B/1162